Storyteller:

a teller of stories
a reciter of tales
liar, fibber

Poetry *is* when an emotion
has found its thought
and the thought has found words.

- Robert Frost

Table of Contents

PART ONE:
Words

PAVEMENT

this is the sort of day
where I'd like to run
— away —
not from anything or anyone
just to something

i see the road
and wonder where it leads
— i want to follow —

bits of gravel
pasted to the earth with tar
"beautiful."
what might happen if I take a step?
could be wonderful
might be my end

definitely would be *something.*

FEET

cold water on bare feet
raging rapids
in a small creek
hairs stand tall
and goosebumbs rise
on pale skin

feeling alive
once again

DAFT

"hope is for children,"
that's what some say.

perhaps it's true
seems to be an idea
built in the days of youth
santa with his reindeer
ballparks and major leagues
pools with crystal clear water

still. i hope.

as an adult
long past my childhood summers
— often —
without apologies
for love. joy. peace.
burritos.

certainly i am daft

for i hope.

KISS

kiss me.
no not like that.
with fresh lips and wild eyes.
let me feel what's been lost for so long.

kiss me.
hmm that's almost right.
but place your hand on my back.
and whisper sweet words of our love.

kiss me.
no that didn't quite work.
run your fingers through my hair.
and sprinkle glitter high above me.

kiss me...

"no. you stop."
"i'm clearly not the one for you."

NO TRADE

i wouldn't change
couldn't exchange
one day of these dark shadows
for a lifetime spent
living in the sunshine

DARKNESS

i sit
in
darkness
so i
can
see.

ARMOR

pulling off my armor
piece by piece
laying it all down
at your feet
until there is nothing
left
but
me
my scarred skin
broken bones
strips of too-thin muscles
holding together what was once
a man

here I am
all of me
as I am
exposed

for you

GIANT

for a moment i was high above
the rest
soaring as if wings were an
afterthought
the world — so blue and green —
filled to the brim with
the quiet
movements
of the grounded ones

i was not them

for a moment
i
was
giant

for a second
i
had
wings

ME

my face was thinner once
my belly
not quite as round
i ate a bit more chicken
a bit less red meat
my feet had blisters from
my running shoes

my years were once less
my goals were once more
the future was anything
everything
i could dream

now here i am

a bit fluffy in places i'm told
to be tight
a bit sadder in ways i'm told
to be glad
a bit less in ways i thought
i'd be more

yet here i am

content in the idea
that i am
finally
perfectly
me

FUTURE FIRE

smooth manicured hands
colored white
with tidy droplets of picketed paint
the same slime everyone uses to brighten
— to blanch —
that barbed wire — wooden line of future fire
in front of rows of oversized dollhouses

the city doesn't deliver
what i need

and nothing out here
wasn't already here
long
before i came

MILK

spoiled milk tastes
fine
if you drink it
all the
time

BROKE & BROKEN

if i get a dollar
spend it
if i get a lover
break it
if i find a shred of happiness
ruin it

for i am man

and man
is a lonely
broken
beast

ALL

you needed more
than i could give
for all i had
was love

STONES AND SKIN

sticks.
stones.
words.
hate.
they all hurt equally the same.

we are all just human after all.
each with soft skin and full hearts.

better to love.
better to give.
better to be better
to each other
in the end.

FRAGILE

peace is such a fragile
wish
and you hold it
with such
ease

NICE GUYS

walks in the sunset
hot coffee and steam
talking about feelings
— love —
listening to people's dreams

poetry and war and peace
both aside his bed
ideas of tomorrow
always spinning in his head

"nice guys finish last,"
they say

and maybe it's true

but at least they finish
somewhere
which is more than some might say
for you

PAPER FISTS

i bring books
to bar fights

AXES AND WINGS

some friends carry
axes
to cut you down
when you grow tall

others fit you
with feathered
wings
to make sure
that you soar

SMOKE

friendship is made
in the fire
and often lost once
the smoke finally
clears

IMPOSSIBLE FUTURE

stuck between
an impossible future
and an unbearable
present,
all I could do was
look to the past.

and there
— once again —
were you.

BUTTERCREAM

i've forgotten most of us
years and days gone by

but still i remember that
short butter-cream dress
and that look of love
in your eyes

HOPE

Hope was beautiful
Hope was fragile
Hope was exquisite

Hope was everything,
When she was mine.

DREAMS

to live in these mornings,
right before the break
of day

to still be lost in
nighttime dreams

to still be swept away

LOUDNESS

it wasn't the noise
— loudness —
or all the careful words
that showed her
his love

it was the quiet
stillness
— his steady gaze —
that proved his heart
was hers

HEARTS AND LIPS

sit with me
in silence
let our hearts say
what our lips
never could

POTIONS

we brought the
same potions
and said the
same words

but this time
there was no
magic

and sadly
no cure

POISON

i agreed
to drink
your poison
and have been
dying ever
since.

L YOU. TELL ME.

        ll you
things
i want to
hear
in hopes
you'll say
the same
to me

LISTEN

i thought i needed to scream
to be heard
— violence
and wretch —

splattering words at the sky
like thick paint

but then
i shut my mouth
and suddenly
— magically —
everyone
listened

SPEAK HEAVY

speak heavy to me
long stocky words
thick syllables
thumping
every letter
with haughty breaths

let me know your
deepest thoughts
your most complex
wonderings
sound them out
clearly
powerfully
to my
listening ears

LIPS AND WORDS

i watched your lips
move like silk
against each other

never once
did i hear a
single word

SEEING

just once
i need you
to look at me
like i
look at you
to know we're
seeing the
same
thing.

EVERYTHING

what was once
my everything
has now become
my nothing
at all

CRACKED PAVEMENT

i stepped quickly on the
cracked pavement path.
i had to be somewhere.
where?
i couldn't say.
for a time I just needed
to be alone.

feet moving forward
mind light of life
free.

no people or conversations,
no wants or needs.
just a quiet
talk with
me.

ALONE

be
alone

and

be
free

SPOIL ME

if you spoil me
may it be with lavish words
long and stretched
full of life and wicked wonder

if you treat me
may it be with plump books
filled to the spine with your
fantastical prose and lines

for your words are all i need

so give them freely
wonderfully
perfectly
to me

DREAM DANCE

true love
never
sleeps...

it dances
in your
dreams.

NOTHING IN THE DARK

pop-tart crumbs cover
my gray t-shirt
giving it a bit of color

i have the curtains pulled
and the lights dimmed low

as I stare into my flashing screens

i should be miserable in the place
— this spot of nothing new —
but i am not
it's quite the opposite

doing nothing in the dark
is exactly what
i want to do

WICKS

light bulbs burn
out

candles waste their
wicks

fire
cools eventually

but my love for you
never will

A LOVE POEM

my heart shattered
when we
first kissed
for i knew
my life
had been
a waste
without
you

HER LIPS

suicide
by her
lips
seemed
the
proper
way
to
go

VILLAINS

time and space...

those are the
real villains.

HAMMERS AND KNIVES

i sleep on a
pile of
hammers and
knives.

each left behind
by someone
no longer in
my life.

                    e end —
                      i.

                         urs — of course —
                    ssions, dreams,
            moments.
out — in the end —
looking back
all of it
all of them
all of everything
that wasn't you

was really not much more
than nothing
at all

and all that nothing
was never enough
to replace that
sweet something
we once had.

HIGH

i never knew
how high
i could fly

until you
let me
go.

POCKETS AND GUNS

she reached into
her pocket
and pulled out
a loaded gun

she shot

i laughed

in the end
we both had fun

SORRYS

i don't trust easy sorrys

casual apologies tossed
across the room
like some sort of cheap
childhood game

if you are sorry
— truly sorry —
prove it

BEAUTIFUL LIE

you were
such
a beautiful
lie

ONCE MINE

she was magic
she was light
she was fury
she was fight
she was beautiful
she was...wonderful
she
was
once
mine.

GHOSTS

your ghost
weighs
heavy
on my
bones

FIGHT THE FOREST

some days i need to
fight the forest.
bloodying my knuckles
against an ancient tree.

to be completely lost
in my quiet rage,
as the rest of the world
fades away.

TIMBER

i yelled as the old tree
fell
its sound concussive
like a bomb

sadly
you did not hear my
cry
and now you're dead
and gone

QUICK THIS NIGHT

come quick this
night,
these needed dreams
of you and i
together.

stay back you
dawn,
you filthy thief.

quick stealing what
i love the most.

HEAT

i miss the weight
of you in my
bed,

the subtle heat
of your body
next to mine.

TENDERED

she tendered
my heart
with her
kiss
and her
fight

MOUNTAIN

i pushed and i
struggled
i fought and i
swore

my knuckles were
bloody
my body was
torn

then you came along
and told me to
stop fighting,
and moved my whole
mountain
with just a few
words

CLIFFS

you lifted me
high
into the air

just to throw
me
off a cliff

SHUT UP

shut up
and love me
or keep talking
and watch me go

LOVE STORY

"anything. everything. just take
what you want," I said.

so she slit my chest open
and ripped out my heart.

YOU SAID

you said you
couldn't
— wouldn't —
live without
me in your
life...

then.
you.
left.

THIS MORNING

come fast this morning
hold tight
this feeling of newness
linger
in this still easy haze
— unafraid of the coming night —

be still here in this quiet
hold gentle the morning dew
stay here
be here
never step into what is next

in this way we will live
forever

you and i
in this
place

EASY

just because
it
comes easy
doesn't mean
it
isn't special

HONESTLY BROKEN

okay...
let's be honest.

at this point
neither of us is changing

so...

Let's just be
broken
together.

HAPPILY

golden bricks and
lollipop kids
our love was once
quite a tale

now we stand
— bathed in
emerald light —
without courage
a heart
or a way
back
home

MOMENT

for a moment
i was
happy,
then i
compared
myself
to you.

LIFETIME OF LOVE

after a
lifetime of
pain and hurt
in the end
all most can
remember
is love

MISTAKES

i would
rather make
mistakes
with love
than find
success
with
harm

MIDNIGHT

she slipped
into
midnight
like a
queen
into a
gown

YOUR LOVE

funny how the one you love
sees you differently

like to whole wide world
pictures you
— views you —
one or two ways

but your love
watches with unique
vision

your faults
your strengths
your everything
different through loves eyes

kind of beautiful
&
kind of strange

ROSE—COLORED

I look at those
rose—colored
lips
and hate
every moment
they were
not mine

YOU SAID

then you said,
"i love you."

and nothing was
ever the same.

PLUCKED

you gave me wings
just to pluck
each feather
from my back
and watch me
crash back
to earth

CHASE

it's not that
i didn't want
to chase you

i just got
tired of
running

DAYS AND SEASONS

skipped stones across a cool
spring pond

firelight on a circle of split
wood — fire chairs

snowflakes on the tips of
wet tongues

and crimson leaves piled high
to the heavens

seasons
how lovely

days
how few

HOME

whether you realize it or not,
home isn't always some far-off
place you come from. most of the
time, it's right in front of your eyes.

— The Organics: Earth

find a copy on AMAZON

or www.TopherWrites.com

CALVIN

it is the echoes of childhood
that keep me sane
glimmers and shimmers
of imagination
that turn the dull into
something more

i'm a bit calvin in that way
always picturing situations
the way i want to see

— life where there isn't —
—adventure where
there might still be —
— spaceships and monsters —
— G.R.O.S.S. —

in the end i will have seen
a bit less REAL than the rest
and spent a bit more time
in my head

but that's how i survive
this mixed up world

with a stuffed tiger
and a red sled

WRITE YOUR POEM ON THIS PAGE
& SHARE IT WITH ME!

@Topher_Writes on instagram
Topher Kearby (writer) on facebook

TAG ME OR MESSAGE ME A PIC OF YOUR POEM AND
I MIGHT SHARE IT!

PART TWO:

Words on Scraps

in the end
love was the death
of me.

but oh my...
it was a beautiful
way to go.

- topher kearby

EVERYTHING

what was once
my everything
has now become
my nothing
at all.

— topher
 kearby

go easy into
your future
if you must.

i will
instead
burn every
bridge and
set my
world on
FIRE.

- topher
  kearby

HIS END

never have i felt this
- touch -
this
- power -
before
beautiful
magical
more perfect than all
the rest
this moment
- one final breath -
before everything becomes
nothing
....
this is all i ever wanted
me with you
here
now - forever -
too bad
it's all too late
my forever
will be done
in a ...

- Topher Kearby

heaven and
hell
on my
shoulders

your name

on my
heart

Topher Earby

"LIES"

your lies were
so good
i didn't trust
the truth
when you finally
spoke it.

— topher kearby

LOUDNESS

it wasn't the noise
- loudness -
or all his careful words
that showed her
his love
it was the quiet
stillness
- his steady gaze -
that proved his heart
was hers

- topher kearby

love is easy.
i mean...
wasn't long ago i fell
deeply in love with a
thin crust pizza.
just cheese.

it's life that's hard.
routine.
the grind.
not enough bump & grind.
(i realize no one says that
anymore but come on...they should)

POINT. let me make it.
love a lot. maybe more
than you get. it's free and
it feels pretty good.

life - if you let it -
will come out and break ya
so add a bit more love to it
and we might all just make it.

ROPHER EARBY

MORNINGS

i love the mornings.
haze of midnight still
heavy on my eyelids —
as if fighting to not
be forgotten.

i am the same;
fighting for someone
in the end to remember
i was here. i lived.

that'd be good.
that'd be enough.
that'd be.

- topher kearby

scattered stars

without a whisper,
a hum,
a breath.
you spoke with the
energy of a thousand
scattered stars.
pulsing,
waiting to explode
and change the universe
forever.

— topher kearby

𝓚

STUFF

the good things in life
- the really good stuff -
you know...
the kind of stuff that
makes your toes curl
and your teeth rattle

that stuff is always a bit
exciting. a bit frightning.
a bit wonderful.
a bit terrible.
a bit everything.

go out and find
that stuff.

- topher kearby

YOU BROKE MY
HEART
   JUST TO
FEEL YOURS
BEAT
ONCE
   AGAIN.

- KOPHER
   EARBY

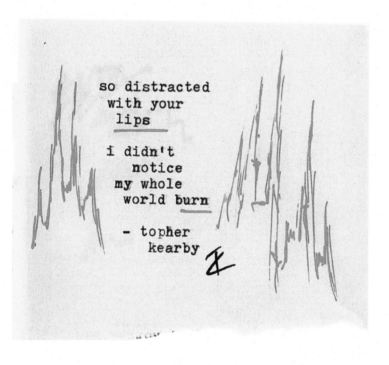

so distracted
with your
 lips

i didn't
   notice
my whole
  world burn

   - topher
     kearby

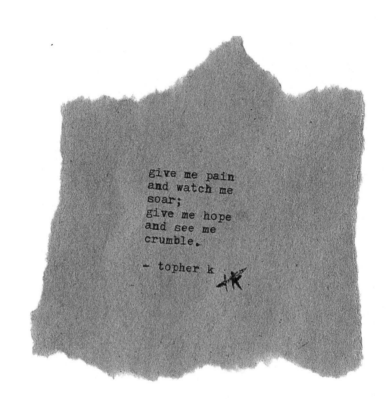

give me pain
and watch me
soar;
give me hope
and see me
crumble.

- topher k

I NEVER
QUESTION
ETERNITY, FOR
I'VE HELD
HEAVEN IN
MY ARMS.

Xopher Earby

```
    it's easy
to spend every second
 of every day
  trying
fighting
    to win
 - acceptance
- love
    - whatever
you can't...
so just be you
  it's easier that way

- topher kearby
```

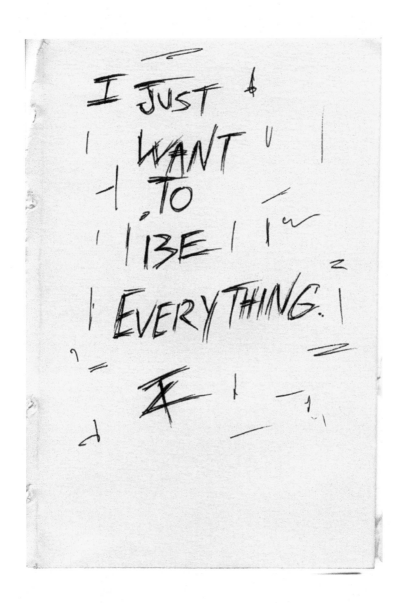

I JUST
WANT
TO
BE
EVERYTHING.

FEAR

fear is an easy
bullet
loaded into the loudest
gun
shot into a crowd of millions
often wielded by just
one

- topher kearby
i. choose, love.

let's not ruin
this moment
with more   forced
words
neither of us needs
to speak
to say what our
hearts have
already said

just shut up
and love me
and i'll do
the same

- Topher K

I HOPE BECAUSE
I STILL HAVE
BREATH..

I BREATHE
BECAUSE
I STILL HAVE
HOPE..

𝔽

the most powerful
response to
hate
is to love more
fear less
do more with this.
life than you
ever dreamed possible
in these ways
we are strong
in these ways we
are free

my heart is with
you Paris
my hope is with
us all

- Topher K

a **KISS**
will answer a
thousand questions
that your words
never could.

— topher kearby

74

i loved you
but not the
way you needed
to be love
so — in the end —
i lost you.

— topher k

𝒦 16

love is many things.
and sometimes it's
Waking up in the
middle of the night
smiling - laughing -
because that one
you love is on your
mind. and life is
good and right.

YOU PULLED
MY LUNGS
THROUGH YOUR
LIPS
AND TOOK
MY BREATH
FROM ME

Zopher
Fearby

"LYRICS"

everyone seems to
be singing the same
song. like they all
were given lyrics.

i just stand and hum
along. moving my lips.
swaying. hoping no one
realizes.

- topher kearby

you never loved me.
you just loved the
idea of "us"

- topher kearby

YOU SEE
    THE THING
    IS I DON'T
    MISS YOU

    AND THAT'S
    WHAT BREAKS
        MY HEART

no.
you have it wrong.
i still believe
in love.

i just don't
believe in
you.

- topher
    kearby

NOTHING AT ALL

i watched the images outside my
window and i was sure they shook.
as if it were all some sort of
strange mirage.
blurred shapes and colors.
time, it wobbled — unsteady.
drunk and stumbling across
my view.

if this isn't real...
what then?
what now?
if "this" isn't the thing
what is?

perhaps all of this is
really nothing
at all.

- topher kearby

"You WROTE
NOVELS WITH
YOUR LIPS,
WITHOUT
SPEAKING
A WORD."

ᵏopHER
EARBY

83

NUMBERS

one. two. three.
four. five.
five fingers curled into
one fist.
two hammers of my flesh
against the red bricks.
three days you've been
away.
four hours i let my knuckles
bleed. crmson staining my
levis.
five years it'll take to
forget you.
five long years until
i'll be dead... AND GONE.

- topher kearby

84

IF THIS
WAS "IT."
- MY ONE SHOT -
I WONDER IF
IT WAS
ENOUGH...

opher EARBY

i never fear a
heartbreak
that searing throbbing
PAIN
no - instead -
i worry for
the time
when i no longer
feel
a thing

- Topher K

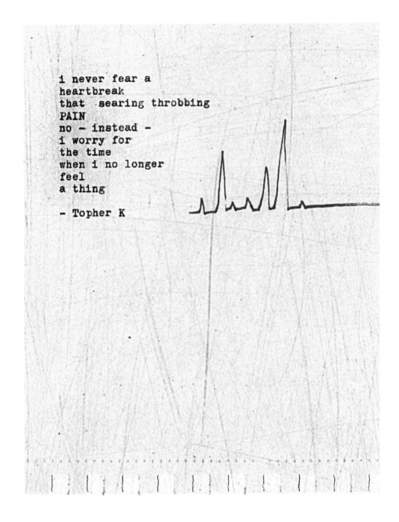

I'll TAKE
THE
PAIN
IF
IT COMES
WITH YOUR
♡ LOVE.

KOPHER
EARBY

i agreed
to drink
your poison
and have been
dying ever
since.

– topher kearby

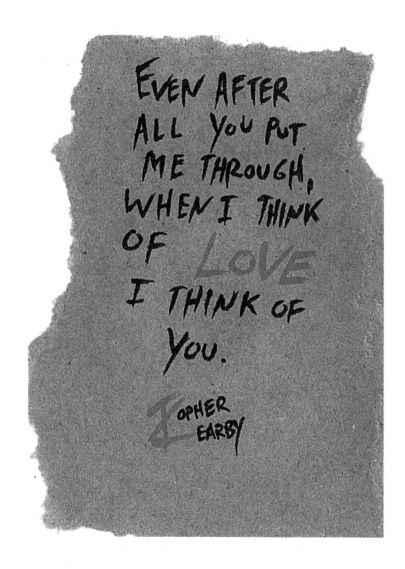

EVEN AFTER
ALL YOU PUT
ME THROUGH,
WHEN I THINK
OF LOVE
I THINK OF
YOU.

ZOPHER
EARBY

rainbows and rocket ships
wooden derby cars
& sandboxes filled with stars

childhood dreams;
how easily i slept back then

now my eyelids rarely shut
too afraid to sleep
to miss brief moments
of this short life

adult. insomniac.

"REAL MEN"
FIGHT & MAKE
WAR
SLITTING' THROATS
TO BE 👑
KING.
I WONDER THEN...
WHAT THAT
MAKES
ME.

F

ROOTS RUN
DEEP
WHEN THE SOIL
IS SOFT
AND EASY,

REACHING FOR A

SOURCE OF

FRESH WATER.

Topher Farby

lay your
secrets
at my <u>feet</u>,

i'll need
them all
to keep
you in
your
place.

— topher
   kearby

let's keep this thing of ours
simple
you love me
i'll love you
and just forget about the
rest

- Topher K

MY HEART SHATTERED
   WHEN WE
   FIRST KISSED
   FOR I KNEW
   MY LIFE
        HAD BEEN
   A WASTE
   WITHOUT YOU.

TOPHER
 EARBY

open doors
are for
quitters.

i brought
a sledgehammer.

- topher kearby

YOUR
TONGUE
SLIT MY
WRISTS

—Kopher
 Earby

"SNAKE OILS"

keep your snake oils
for yourself,
what i got don't
need a cure.

'cause ain't nothin'
wrong with being broken.
of that one thing
i'm sure.

Topher Earby

WE ALL NEED
SOMETHING
WE CAN'T
HAVE,
FOR ME
THAT SOMETHING
IS
YOU.

FEARBY
TOPHER

she was stardust
in a bottle;

an entire universe
waiting to be
born.

Kopher Earby

A faint glimmer of light trickles through my
bedroom window. Maybe it's a little sad that
such a small slice of sunshine makes me smile,
but it's been a while - a long while since any
light made it through those thin panes of glass.
You see...this is the end. Not of this day, though
it is getting a bit late, or event this month or
this year. No. Itx is THE END.

Of everything.

How then am I reading this letter? You may be
asking yourself. Well, I'll start by saying,
"I have no clue. Youx see, X&X I8m already dead."
spoiler alert But I8d wager a guess that this
letter is already quite old and you have stumbled
upon it in an area that was once booming and pulsing
with life and energy. Now what is it...I wonder.

SORRY, I got distracted. Why write such a letter on
what is certainly my last day? Well, I do it simply
for one reason. - X&X it's quite a selfish reason *
I must admit and normally I might apologize, but
not today. You see I want you to remember me, through
these few words typedquickly on cheap paper. I want
your eyes to drink in each letter and your mind to
quietly wonder: Who was this strange man who lived
where I now walk. What good did he do before his time
was finally up?
Honestly? I have no great boasts to leave behind. I
was simply a man, but none of that quite matters today.
Because, this is my end and I simply want you to know:
I was once here and I8m terrified of being alone...

i did the thing
i swore i'd never
do...

i went and fell
in love with
you.

- topher kearby

TEARS AND SCARS

looking quickly, you'd see my tears as pain
- pools of unresolved hurt -
lingering against my cheeks
like wet sorrow
a glistening of sadness
drenching my skin with thick damp anguish

but see, you'd be wrong
these tears
brilliant and blistering
are the salve that seals my wounds
- transforming them into beautful scars -
healing my mind with each gentle drop
sanding smooth my coarse memories

so...do not see these tears as pain
see them as i do
- as power -
to live
to breathe
to move the hell on
to be finally
perfectly
me

"TRUE JOY"

```
true joy is
giving what can't
be   gotten
from anyone
other than
you

- topher k.
#goodnight
```

"YOU'RE NOT THE SAME
PERSON YOU ONCE WERE,"
SHE SAID.

"AND YOU HAVEN'T
CHANGED A BIT,"
HE REPLIED... AS HE
WALKED AWAY.

TOPHER EARBY

WHEN I
FOUND
MY
WINGS
YOU
BECAME
SO SMALL

you and me.
let's drink until
our eyes shut tight,
kiss until our
lips quake and tremble,
laugh until each of
our breaths are empty.

you and i.
let's fall in love.

— topher kearby

LIE TO ME....
I CAN TAKE
THAT.
JUST DON'T TELL
ME
THE TRUTH.

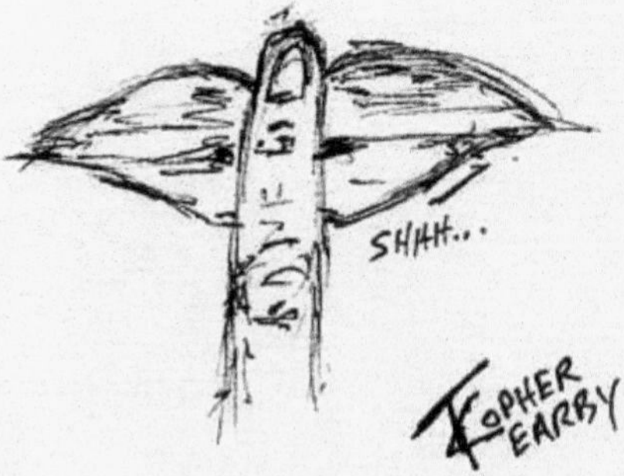

LAY ON MY COUCH
TELL ME YOUR
    HEARTACHE $
    LET THE NUMBERS
    CLIMB $
    ON MY
        LEDGER.
    $ $ $

        $

WRITE / SKETCH YOUR POEM ON THIS PAGE
& SHARE IT WITH ME!

@Topher_Writes on instagram
Topher Kearby (writer) on facebook

TAG ME OR MESSAGE ME A PIC OF YOUR POEM AND
I MIGHT SHARE IT!

PART THREE

Words on Art

113

she was
coffee
and
        stardust.

            — topher
            kearby

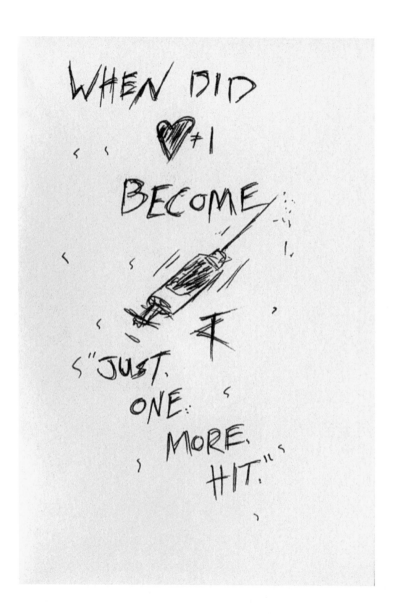

115

FIRST STEPS

THE JOURNEY WAS LONG
SCATTERED DAYS ADDING TOGETHER
TO FORM A LENGTH OF TIME UNIMAGINED
WHEN THE FIRST STEP WAS TAKEN

WOULD YOU DO IT AGAIN
STANDING AT THE START
LOOKING NO LONGER
AT THE GOAL
BUT AT THE WORK
INVOLVED TO REACH
YOUR DESTINATION

COULD YOU TAKE
THAT FIRST STEP
KNOWING THE END
WOULD BE SO FAR
SO MUCH LONGER
THAN YOU PLANNED

BETTER NOT TO KNOW
THE PRICE PAID
FOR ACCOMPLISHMENT
INSTEAD KNOW
THAT WHATEVER
THE COST

THE JOURNEY
ON ITS OWN
WAS WORTH IT

- TOPHER KEARBY

116

flowers fade
and wilt
and die
but damn
aren't they
beautiful
just for
that short
while...

- topher
  kearby

117

feathered arrow &
tightened string,
cupid plunged
his arrow
deep.

KOPHER
EARBY

danger
is
beautiful

119

EVERYBODY
IS SINGING
THE SAME
SONG
AND I'M
JUST SWAYING,
HUMMING
ALONG

she only wanted
flowers
taken from
the cemetery

said it made
her feel
alive

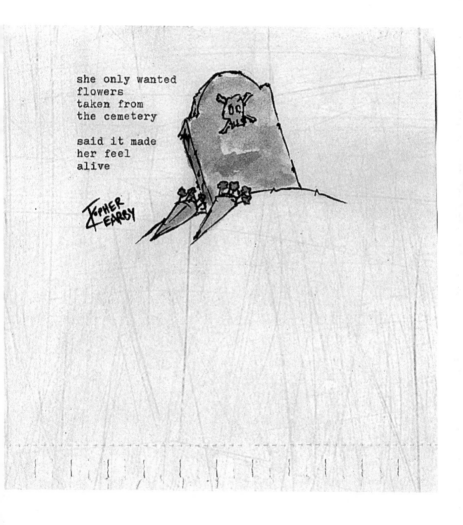

all he ever
wanted was
her happiness
so even though
his heart was
broken —
he smiled as
  she walked
   away.

122

for the first
time in forever
her future
was her own.

and she was
not going to
waste a moment.

124

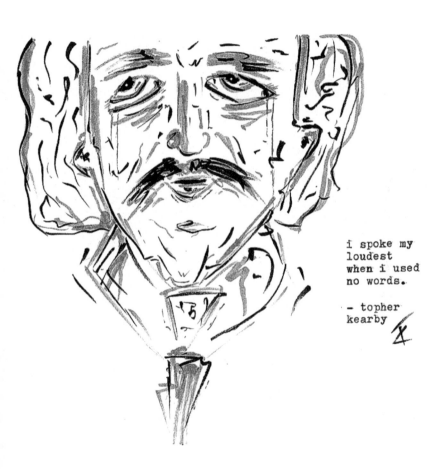

i spoke my
loudest
when i used
no words.

- topher
kearby

125

our love
- like a Polaroid -
just took a little
time to develop

ESTHER EARBY

126

life is an easy
kind of
HOPE
when you're
standing
hand-in-hand
with me.

- topher
  kearby

127

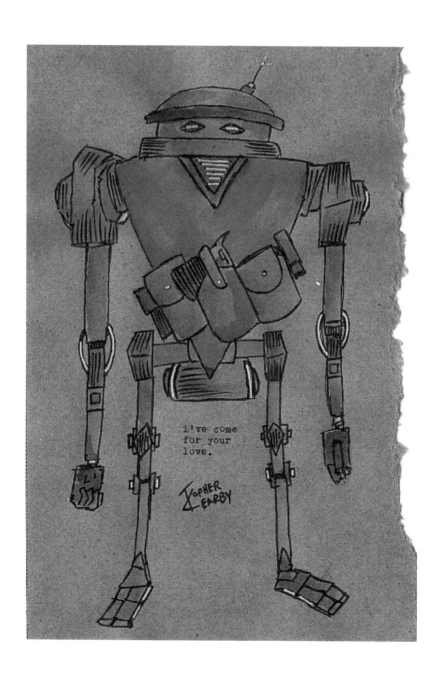

i've come
for your
love.

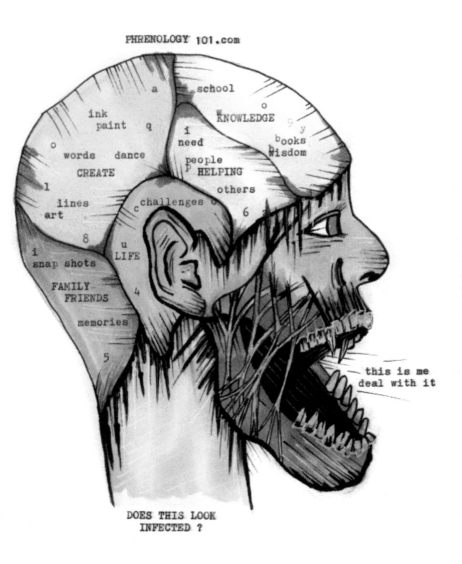

PHRENOLOGY 101.com

a
school
ink
paint q
KNOWLEDGE
o
w
o
i
y
words dance
need
books
CREATE
people
b
wisdom
HELPING
l
P
others
lines
challenges
art
c o
6
8
u
LIFE
i
snap shots
FAMILY
FRIENDS
4
memories
5

this is me
deal with it

DOES THIS LOOK
INFECTED ?

129

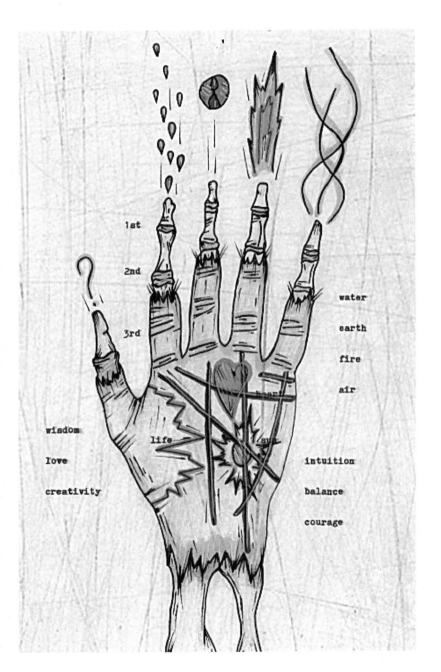

1st

2nd

3rd

water

earth

fire

air

wisdom

life

heart

sun

intuition

love

balance

creativity

courage

131

grip tight
the thorns
let each tip
pierce your
skin
while you breathe
the bitter aroma
of the dying
beauty

— topher k

SOFT LIPS
RATTLE
MY
BONES.

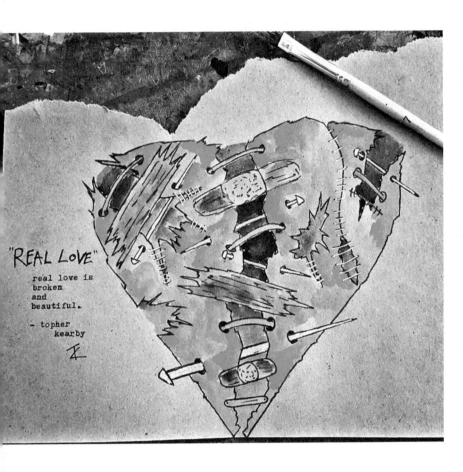

"REAL LOVE"

real love is
broken
and
beautiful.

- topher
  kearby

ONE IDEA

that moment - a flash of light
a single idea - so good...powerful
that it can't help but change
everything

an invisible BLAST
of energy
that blows
your mind
and makes
every
struggle
every
drop of pain
totally
&
completely
worth it

- Topher Kearby

LIE TO ME....
    I CAN TAKE
        THAT.
    JUST DON'T TELL
        ME
        THE TRUTH.

SHHH...

KOPHER EARBY

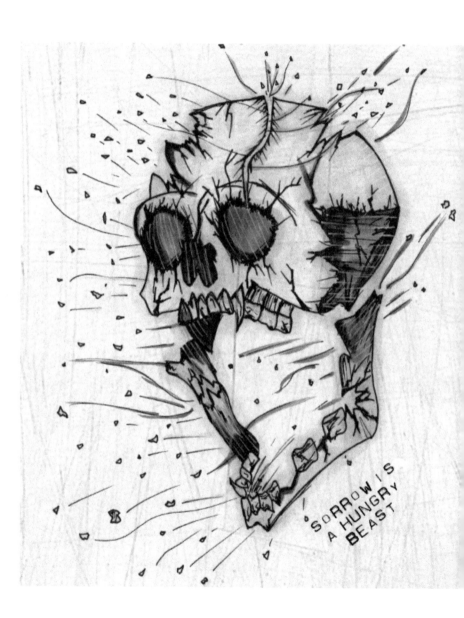

138

i shake   when i feel you

SEE
ME
AS
I <u>AM</u>
NOT AS
YOU WANT
ME TO
<u>BE</u>..

LIFE IS WHAT
WE LEAVE BEHIND

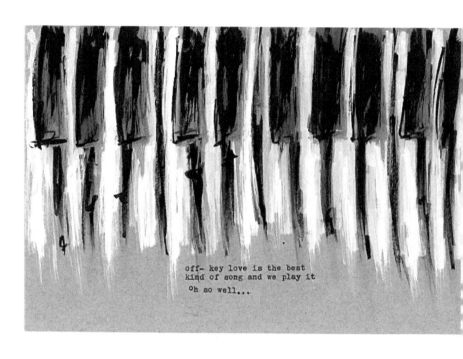

off- key love is the best
kind of song and we play it
Oh so well...

fill the
world with
wonderful
words.
for they may
be all we
have.

Xopher
EARBY

143

i see you
worry about
my smoke
when you
should really
fear my
FIRE.

- top_{her k.}

144

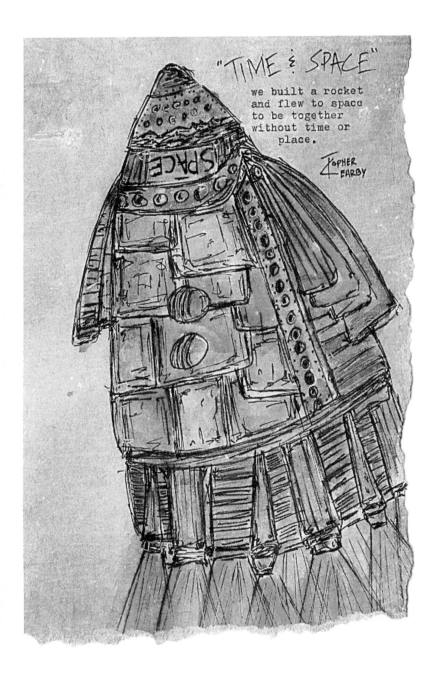

"TIME & SPACE"

we built a rocket
and flew to space
to be together
without time or
place.

Zopher Farby

145

i didn't ask
for this
i didn't want it
but now it's
who i am...

- topher kearby

146

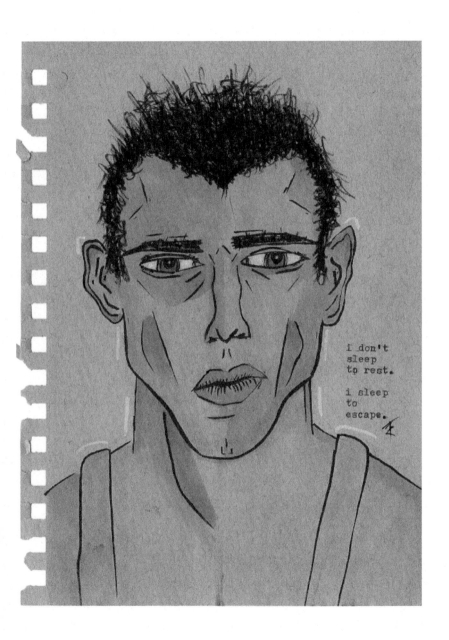

147

beauty is
endangered

149

our only
true home
was in
the stars

- Topher

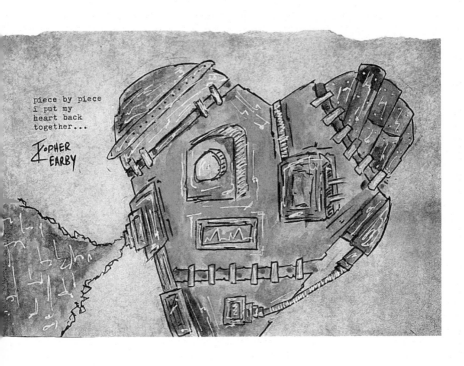

piece by piece
i put my
heart back
together...

KOPHER
EARBY

151

PEOPLE WILL
VIEW YOU
WITH THEIR
OWN EYES
BUT DON'T
LET THEIR
PERSPECTIVE
CHANGE YOUR
SIGHT
FOR YOU

- TOPHER K

Let's go on
an adventure.

"MISTAKES"
i've been
too good
my whole
life,
it's time
for more
mistakes.

KOPHER
EARBY

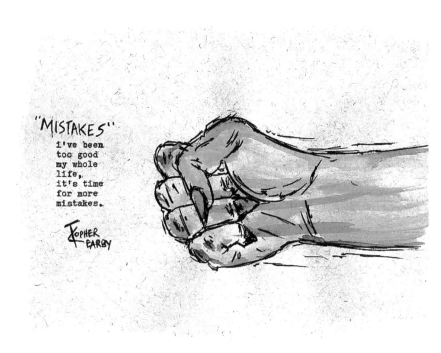

my voice
is strong
my words
are fierce
i cannot
i will not
be silent

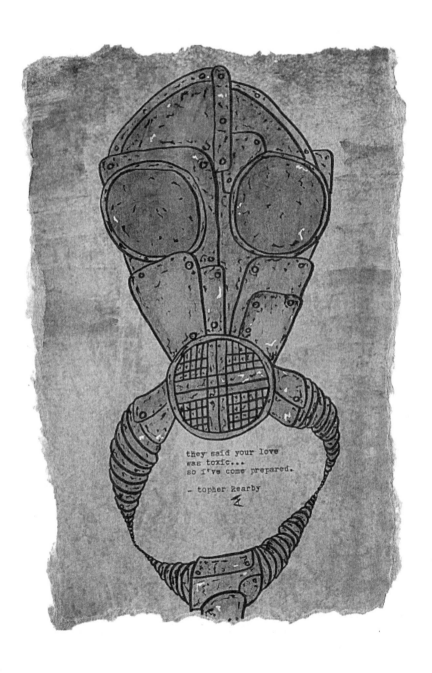

they said your love
was toxic...
so i've come prepared.

— topher kearby

157

BEAUTIFUL STORIES

COME OUT OF
TERRIBLE MESSES

TOPHER KEARBY

STRENGTH

IS

BEAUTY

fierce
& wild,
watch me
soar.

as if
i ever
needed
wings
to
fly

topher kearby

THIS IS
HOW
IT
ENDS.

SKETCH SOMETHING ON THIS PAGE
& SHARE IT WITH ME!

@Topher_Writes on instagram
Topher Kearby (writer) on facebook

TAG ME OR MESSAGE ME A PIC OF YOUR SKETCH
AND I MIGHT SHARE IT!

THE ORGANICS: CINDER — FREE PREVIEW
(available on Amazon, TopherWrites.com & other
retailers worldwide)

CHAPTER 1: CLUE

WHATEVER was left of Taurin's youth ended the day the crimson flecks appeared in his eyes. Most people turn their backs on the boy, save for Pulp and Violet, and even his own father, weary from a lifetime of struggle, has little to do with him now. Taurin has been marked without warning or explanation. Hiding among the forest trees that cloak the Temple of Light, he hopes to find out why.

Taurin reaches into his pocket and pulls out a crumpled piece of paper.

It's time to meet. Be at the temple at dusk.

He's read the words a hundred times, and still they haven't changed. So, where is Clue?

Why hadn't Clue shown up himself? He'd been the one who told Taurin where to be and when. Could it be another riddle? Clue had given such short notice this time that if there really was a hidden message, Taurin didn't have time to figure it out.

Clue. It is a fitting name for someone who seems obsessed with hiding the true meaning of his messages. Like when a slab of wood came with a note that read, *Burn bright with flesh. Light the night.* It was by pure accident that Taurin had set the scrap on fire, that he'd become so frustrated flames leapt from his hands. Clue had been leaving Taurin all kinds of things: scraps of wood; three spoiled apples; a swatch of fabric ripped down the center. At first Taurin dismissed them as a joke. But each had proven to be something more.

That's why today's letter is so strange.

Taurin wads the note in a ball and pushes it back into his pocket. For a moment he considers uncovering his speeder and blazing a trail home, leaving behind all of Clue's strange letters and returning to the boring life he had before the crimson flecks had appeared in his eyes.

"Be brave," Taurin mumbles, deciding to move forward. In front of him, slivers of moonlight reveal thick green vines that strangle the temple's stone bricks. Roots, thick and wild, break through nearly every slab of dirt and stone in sight. The Temple of Light looks nothing like its name implies.

Onward still, his woven sandals reach the first step of the winding stairway leading to the temple door. There are nearly twenty more to climb, each cracked and crumbling. Taurin curls his fingers into fists. He's never been in an actual fight before, other than the occasional wrestling match with his brother, Pulp, but if something went wrong, he'd improvise. His long strides carry him to the top of the stairs where a wooden doorway, splintered and rotten, sits directly in front of him. He grabs the metal handle with trembling hands. One quick pull swings it wide.

"Hello?" Taurin whispers. "Anyone here?" Silence. Not a bulb or candle is lit. The dank smell of wilted paper and musky leather fills his nose. *Creepy.*

Trying to concentrate, Taurin looks down at his hand. He's done this before, but never under such pressured circumstances. The lone image of a roaring fire burns in his mind, and within seconds, sparks spring from his palm and grow into dancing flames. "Never gets old," he says, smiling.

Orange light spills into the small room, shining through the darkness. Taurin searches the piles of spoiled books and toppled shelves, but turns up nothing of interest. Then, just as he's about to give up, something strange snags his attention: a pale-blue, almost pulsing light beckons him from across the room. It must have been there all along. Or had it? Inching forward, mindful of his surroundings, Taurin stops as soon as he can see it—a thin glass object resting against a tall stack of books. As long as his hand and twice as wide, it remains entirely transparent except for five strange symbols that shimmer in its center. He's never seen anything like it.

Boom! A rumble, low and full, fills the temple air, vibrating until it rattles deep inside Taurin's bones. Tiny pebbles bounce like insects against cracked tile. Dust shakes loose from the ancient walls.

Watch Force. Taurin couldn't be more certain.

The flame in his hand vanishes, leaving only the blue glow to light the room. Without hesitation, he grabs the pulsing object and throws his body flat against the floor; if he could melt into the cracks, he would. Instead, the boy slithers beneath a stack of dusty books, doing his best to hide. Fiery fists or not, the Watch Force would make quick work of him.

A moment later, a steady yellow beam scans the room inch by inch. A black gloved hand grips tight the polished, metal flashlight from which the light shines. "I could probably take *one*," mumbles Taurin, and for a second fights the urge to rush the dark figure, tackle him against the temple floor, and ignite the soft tissue of his throat. Instead, he swallows a deep gulp of pride; if he couldn't even wrestle Pulp to the ground, how'd he expect to do it to a grown man?

167

Still, he couldn't just wait around for them to find him. Where there was one patrolman there would be another. Where there were two there would be three. For all Taurin knew, there could be ten. Knowing something must be done, he slides the glass tablet into his leather bag, stretches out his hands, and presses them against the tile floor. "Here goes nothing," he murmurs and squeezes his eyes shut.

Rolling fire fills the boy's mind, bones rattle inside quivering skin, and soon, a thin stream of fire pours from his fingertips. Taurin's eyes open and he can see a burning line snaking toward a stack of splintered shelves. Like a match tossed into a stack of dry leaves, they burst into flames, causing the patrolman to stumble backward.

Firelight exposes the black helmet and visor that covers the intruder's head and face. A red WF is stitched onto what looks like the front pocket of a tailored suit jacket. Pleated pant legs disappear into tall black boots that are laced to just below his knees. Gripped tightly in one hand is the flashlight; the other wields a heat pistol. He isn't here just to look around—he's come for Taurin.

Without hesitation, the patrolman hurries out the entrance of the temple, slamming the door behind him. Taurin doesn't have time to think. Swaying flames become a rampant blaze, inching closer to him with every passing second. The fire was meant to be the boy's ticket to an easy escape. Now it looks like it may be his ruin.

He kicks the wall behind him. Small bits of rock and dust fall and scatter on the floor. The inferno has spread out of control, and if he doesn't act soon, Taurin will be boiled alive. Improvising, he lets loose a flurry of fists that smash against the stacked stone. Blood spills from his knuckles, but he keeps hammering away until the small crack grows into an opening just large enough for him to crawl out of.

He shoves his body through the hole, ripping his gray, cotton shirt on the jagged pieces of rock. Taking a quick breath, he tucks the torn fabric back into his jeans and sprints ahead into the forest. A familiar collection of bent branches and piled leaves remind him when to stop. He can almost feel the growl of his ash speeder beneath the greenery. He brushes off the leaves, moves the branches, and positions the machine upright. It's just as he left it—rusted and beautiful.

Taurin tosses his leg over the seat, fires up the ignition, and twists the throttle all the way forward. Within seconds, his speeder is screaming through the tangled vines and crooked branches of the forest path. These broken-down roadways are said to be cursed, filled with unseen dangers, but Taurin has spent enough time exploring them to know the real threat is the roadways themselves. Normally, he would take the time to navigate them properly, but right now that's a luxury he can't afford. The Watch Force move like ghosts in the night. Nobody knows the reason for their actions because they rarely leave anyone to talk about them. The few who have lived through an encounter keep their mouths shut. If forced to choose, Taurin would prefer to be one of the latter.

Focus, he tells himself. You *can make it home.*

A piercing beam of light explodes in front of him. Blinded, he has no other choice but to slide to a stop. He gulps and places his hand to his chest as his worn rubber tires just miss the splintered tree trunk in front of him.

Taurin thought he knew the best paths through the forest, but maybe he was wrong. The Watch Force found him with ease. Did Clue tip them off? Was he followed? The boy pulls his speeder behind a thick tree trunk and sinks a sandaled foot into the loose dirt; he relaxes the other on the speeder's metal footrest. The Watch Force haven't seen him, and he'd like to keep it that way. One wrong move could cost him everything.

Steam rises from the chrome tail pipes of the six ash speeders blocking the path ahead. The familiar red letters *WF* stand out against the matte black finish of their fuel tanks. If there was any doubt in Taurin's mind who was after him before, there isn't now.

Silence sweeps through the forest. The once-thundering engines are now idle. Taurin peers through the shadows, watching the patrolmen dismount their speeders. Black boots push deep into white ash. Metal rifles press hard against firm shoulders. The patrolmen are hunting on foot.

A metallic taste swims up Taurin's throat, but he gulps it back down and readies himself for action. With the flip of a switch, his speeder's headlight floods the path with light. The patrolmen shield their eyes for only a moment, but it's long enough for him to make his move.

He smashes the throttle forward, spinning the tires and spraying dirt in every direction. His speeder weaves around the hunters and covers them in dust and debris, but to Taurin's surprise, they don't fire a single shot in his direction. Instead, they stand like statues in the middle of the trail and watch as he disappears into the forest. As strange as it may be, he can't help but smile. Had he really met the Watch Force and survived?

"Violet's never going to believe this!" he says.

CHAPTER 1: NEW HOME

GROVES of thick trees dripping with emerald leaves stretch as far as the eyes can see. Fat vines, full of life, dangle like plump serpents from their twisted branches. Bright beams of orange and yellow light shine through the dense lid of the forest. A soft breeze blows through crooked rows of ancient trees, cooling the travelers as they pass beneath them. Dry deserts and onyx-colored mountains are long gone. This new land isn't anything like Cinder—nothing like the travelers' home.

Taurin's unkempt strands of brown hair flop and twist as he turns to look behind him. The mighty tree that brought him and his friends to this place remains unchanged. Rigid and unmoved, it stands silent as if not having played a role in any of this—innocent. But Taurin knows better. Bark, black as coal and hard as stone, wraps around the tree's trunk, which stretches ten feet wide and stands over fifty feet high. In Cinder, this would have been the tallest tree in any forest; here it's just one of many. Still, this wooden giant is unique. Locked inside the darkness is a secret—one so long forgotten that almost no one remembered to keep it.

The gateway that brought Taurin and his friends to this world is shut once more, no longer spinning with lights of blue and green. The secret revealed itself just long enough for the travelers to step through from the other side. Closing the gate was Violet's responsibility, though she'll never know. How could she? Every step is a mystery in this strange place, each choice a riddle waiting to be solved.

+++++

Slurping, sucking noises ring out as Shrift pulls his knee-high leather boots from a patch of thick mud. "Ain't got much patience for this stuff," he says. A large clump of damp dirt falls from his boot as he shakes it. "I'd rather be back home than deal with this muck. Least the Wasteland never tried to steal my boots."

"Home tried to steal more than a pair of old boots," Taurin says. "I remember a beast or two that would make this mud look like a reward."

"Don't go flapping your lips too quick. Who knows what's waiting for us behind those trees," Shrift says, his voice hushed. "None of us knows nothin' 'bout this place." He snaps his head back and shouts, "RAWR!"

Shocked, Taurin, Violet, and Echo all tumble backwards in unison. Shrift, pleased with himself, leans back and unleashes a deep belly laugh that shakes the forest. "Ha! That was too easy."

Violet reaches over and punches Shrift's right shoulder. "I'm not going to let your stupidity get the rest of us killed. Not tonight, at least."

"If death wants me so bad, let her come already." Shrift's eyes narrow as he rubs his throbbing shoulder. "Got a feeling just a whole lot of pain and misery are waiting for us beyond those pines. Nothin' ever changes. Especially the bad." He fires a wet glob of spit from his mouth, and it splatters against the ground.

Echo presses her thin fingers against Shrift's chest. "Please, do not speak for all of us," she whispers. "This place offers far more than pain. If we are open, it may reveal a way for us each to find a new beginning."

"She's right," Violet says. "No need to be foolish. Let's make camp here and wait out the dark."

Taurin nods in agreement. The glowing gate has brought him and the others to this place. Whatever waits beyond the tall trees and deep mud of this forest is something they are meant to find—or, at the very least, something they must attempt to understand. There is no turning back; the gate was apparently a one-way ticket.

After walking for a while more, Shrift plops down and rests his back against the rough bark of a tree. "This is as bad a spot as any, I guess. Probably a thousand things that can kill us in this forest. At least here, the mud isn't up to our knees anymore."

"That's the spirit," Violet says, rolling her eyes. "Might as well make the best of—"

"Shhhh." Taurin puts a single finger against his lips. "Do you feel that?"

"I don't feel nothing," Shrift says. "Must have hit your head, or maybe you're just losin' it."

"I feel it too," Echo whispers. "I also see it. Out there." She points toward the edge of the tree line.

Shrift reaches down and places his hand against the wooden handle of his heat pistol. His index finger glides across the hand-carved etchings until it finds what it was searching for—the sickled trigger. "If something wants a fight, I'll be ready," he says.

One torch shines in the dimming light of the forest. Then, two. Finally, more and more appear until a circle of fire surrounds Taurin, Violet, Shrift, and Echo. "You weren't invited," a strong voice booms from the distance. "Leave."

Taurin holds his hands in front of his face to block the light. "We don't want trouble."

"Speak for yourself." Shrift stands, unholsters his heat pistol, and takes aim at one of the flickering flames. "Trouble is all I want."

A single burning arrow rips through the night sky. Its blue flame twists and turns until the jagged metal tip pierces the wet ground just inches from Shrift's boot. A dark beast moves forward from the shadows. Thick mats of brown hair cover every inch of the massive creature, save for a pair of piecing green eyes that shimmer in the darkness. Sharp, curved claws stretch from its four paws and its hot breath spills onto Shrift's face as it draws nearer.

A girl who looks no older than Violet sits perched on its back. Blonde hair, twisted into thick braids, flows down the entire length of her back. A gray pelt forms a heavy coat over her torso, and tight, brown leather pants cover her long legs. Her cream-colored skin is painted with three red stripes across her face, each one the width of a single finger. With both hands, she grips a wooden spear that is longer than she is tall. She brushes its metal tip against Shrift's cheek. "So, you're looking for trouble?"

"I was, but I'd settle for you." Shrift flashes a wide, bright smile. "Why don't you step down from whatever that thing is and chat with me and my friends?"

She flashes a matching smile back at Shrift—paired with a brief chuckle. "Wouldn't be fair. You see," she says as she turns her head, "you haven't met *my* friends."

Three more beasts step out of the shadows. Matted strands of dark hair partially cover their bright green eyes and crooked rows of razor-sharp teeth. They are each somewhat larger than the first, and from the sounds of their snarls, more ferocious.

Three young, male riders sit on the backs of the creatures. The first wears a mask made from a wolf's pelt—his blue eyes peer from where the animal's once did. His thin chest is bare except for three black stripes painted across his flat stomach. Blonde hair covers the second rider's shoulders and back. His strong cheekbones frame his bright-blue eyes and a square chin. Thick muscle covers his arms and legs, and his tight stomach is painted with the same black stripes as the first.

The third rider is short and plump like a pumpkin. He wears an oversized turtle shell for a helmet that sits awkwardly atop his head. A leather strap holds it tight against his round face, pinching his chubby cheeks. His belly, painted the same as the other two, jiggles and sloshes as his beast strides toward the travelers. "I am Soe," the plump boy says. He beats his fist three times against his chest. "You are trespassers."

Taurin steps forward. "We can explain." The sharp tip of Soe's long spear presses against his throat, stopping his movement. Crimson flecks burn in his blue eyes. His fingers twitch with a wild energy. *Be strong*, he thinks. *Be smart.*

Soe pushes the spear harder against Taurin's throat and twists it against his skin. "I'd rather you bleed."

"Brother," the female rider says. "Look at his eyes."

The plump boy pulls his weapon back and locks his gaze on Taurin. For a few long moments he studies him. Then, he scratches his belly with his short, chubby fingers and speaks. "Organic?"

The word sounds strange to Taurin. He's heard it before, but to hear it spoken from a stranger is unsettling. He doesn't answer. Terrible things happen when people discover his secret. Better to stay silent.

Speak the truth. Echo's voice resounds in Taurin's mind. *You do not need to hide. Not any longer.*

"I asked you a question." The other two male riders move next to Soe and aim at Taurin with their wooden spears. "I expect an answer."

Taurin steps back. His black boots sink and twist in the wet slog, but his balance isn't lost. He turns his palm upward and stretches it toward Soe. "Burn bright. Ignite the night," he whispers. A red flame grows from his hand and shines on those gathered. With a sweeping motion, he tosses the fire up into the sky and, like a firework, its red and orange colors dance in the darkness.

"There's your answer," Shrift says. His smile shimmers in the fading light. "'Fraid we can't help you if you need more than that." His fingers tap the handle of his heat pistol. "Catch my drift?"

The girl slides off her beast and walks toward Shrift. "There won't be a need for that." With a flick of her wrist, she pulls Shrift's pistol from its holster and slams it against the ground without laying a finger on the weapon. Purple flecks sparkle in her eyes. "My name is Lewren. Sorry for trouble, but we don't get many visitors. Especially ones that don't want to harm us. My brother can be a bit protective." She looks back to the pudgy boy, still seated atop his beast. "I vouch for them."

"Then you are responsible for their choices and actions. Whatever trouble or chaos they bring is on your head," Soe grunts. He wobbles one of his stubby fingers at Shrift. "I don't trust the big one."

"Feeling is shared, friend," Shrift says. He bends down and picks up his heat pistol and gives it a quick shake to knock the wet dirt that covers the barrel and grip loose. Then he slides it back into the leather holster on his side. "I'll forgive that one mistake, darlin', but the next time I won't be so generous."

Lewren steps toward Shrift. "I'm no one's *darlin'*." She presses a small knife against his belly. "Understand?"

"More than you know, darl—"

Lewren's face turns red. "I said …"

"Ha," Shrift laughs, "didn't peg you as the jumpy type."

Violet shakes her head and steps between the pair. "If you two are done flirting, we really should get moving."

"I'd never flirt with that oaf." Lewren glares at Violet as she slides the knife back in her pocket. "But you're right. We need to get out of here before the others find us."

"Others?" Taurin asks.

"No time to explain," Lewren says, then she mounts her beast with ease and turns it to face the forest. "Follow us if you want to keep your skin."

Taurin shrugs. It wouldn't be his first idea to follow a group of armed strangers into the depths of a dark and potentially dangerous forest, but right now, it's his only choice. He turns to his friends and says, "Let's go."

ADAMFARSTER.COM
Illustration & Graphic Design

CPSIA information can be obtained
at www.ICGtesting.com
Printed in the USA
LVOW06s2259230217

525301LV00047B/874/P